Platform
Papers

Quarterly essays from Currency House   No. 10: October 2006

CURRENCY HOUSE

PLATFORM PAPERS
Quarterly essays from Currency House Inc.

Editor: Dr John Golder, j.golder@unsw.edu.au

Currency House Inc. is a non-profit association and resource centre advocating the role of the performing arts in public life by research, debate and publication.

Postal address: PO Box 2270, Strawberry Hills, NSW 2012, Australia

Email: info@currencyhouse.org.au   Tel: (02) 9319 4953
Website: www.currencyhouse.org.au   Fax: (02) 9319 3649

Executive Officer: Polly Rowe

Editorial Board: Katharine Brisbane AM, Dr John Golder, John McCallum, Greig Tillotson

ISBN 0 97573 016 9
ISSN 1449-583X

Cover design by Kate Florance, Currency Press
Typeset in 10.5 Arrus BT
Printed by Hyde Park Press, Adelaide

This edition of Platform Papers is supported by donations from the following: the Keir Foundation, Katharine Brisbane, Malcolm Duncan, David Marr, Tony Scotford, Alan Seymour, Greg and Fiona Quirk, Mary Vallentine and Jane Westbrook. To them and to all our supporters Currency House extends sincere gratitude.

Contents

AVAILABILITY Platform Papers, quarterly essays on the performing arts, is published every January, April, July and October and is available through bookshops or by subscription. For order form, see page 80.

LETTERS Currency House invites readers to submit letters of 400–1,000 words in response to the essays. Letters should be emailed to the Editor at j.golder@unsw.edu.au or info@currencyhouse.org.au, or posted to Currency House at PO Box 2270, Strawberry Hills, NSW 2012, Australia. To be considered for the next issue, the letters must be received by 9 November 2006.

CURRENCY HOUSE For membership details, see our website at: www.currencyhouse.org.au

Satire— or Sedition?

The Threat to National Insecurity

JONATHAN BIGGINS

The author

JONATHAN BIGGINS is a writer, performer and broadcaster. Since beginning his career at the Hunter Valley Theatre Company, he has worked for all the state theatre companies, in productions ranging from David Williamson's *Soulmates* to *West Side Story*. In 2003 he made his debut with Opera Australia in *Orpheus in the Underworld*, for which he also co-wrote a new adaptation of the libretto, and in 2004 he played Koko in *The Mikado*. He has hosted the afternoon ABC radio shift for Sydney's 702, co-written and performed in *Three Men and a Baby Grand* for ABC-TV and hosted *Critical Mass*, the ABC-TV's weekly arts programme. As director of Revue for the Sydney Theatre Company, he has featured in (among others) the sell-out *Sunday in Iraq with George*, *Much Revue About Nothing* and *Fast and Loose*. He wrote a fortnightly column for Fairfax's *Good Weekend* magazine and earlier this year his first book, *As It Were*, was published by ABC Books.

Author's acknowledgements

I should like to thank Peter Pinne for permission to use his four-part history of the Phillip Street Theatre, 'It Didn't Always Close on Saturday Night', *On Stage*, 6.2 (Autumn 2005)–7.1 (Summer 2006) and Robina Beard, for allowing me to read 'A Narrative History of the Phillip Street Theatre (1954–1963)' (unpublished Master of Creative Arts thesis, University of Wollongong, 1994). Thanks are also due to Robyn Nevin, Rob Brookman, Stephen Armstrong and Max Gillies for permission to quote from interviews they were good enough to give me, and to my colleagues Drew Forsythe, Phil Scott and Linda Nagle for their permission to reproduce scripts which they co-authored. Finally, I should like to acknowledge the generous contribution of all the actors and musicians who have been involved in the *Wharf Revue* over the years, and to all the people at the Sydney Theatre Company who have lent us their unflagging support.

To the other two-thirds of the *Wharf Revue*,
Drew Forsythe and Phil Scott.
And to Ruth, the fourth musketeer.

Foreword

This essay is about the role of theatrical satire in contemporary Australia. It is by no means a comprehensive analysis of the state of political writing for the stage in this country, but rather an account of the personal experience of a creator and performer of satirical revue. More specifically, it recounts the history of the Sydney Theatre Company's *Wharf Revue*—why and how it began and, particularly, the manner in which, over its six-year lifespan since 2000, it has evolved from broad, knockabout cabaret to exclusively political satire.

Australians have a long and healthy history of respectful disrespect for their social institutions and political leaders, underpinned by a general tolerance born of egalitarianism. In fact, to borrow the logic of Joseph Heller, it has long been un-Australian to use the term 'un-Australian'. Revue, emerging as it did from the populist traditions of the music hall and vaudeville, reflected a national ability to laugh at oneself. In many ways, political revue is the theatrical equivalent of the great Australian symbol of irreverence, the black-and-white political cartoon. One might legitimately ask how that has come about. What is so appealing about revue as a dramatic form that has ensured the ongoing vitality of this venerable genre? Is the theatre really the best place for effective, topical satire, given the ability of radio and television to present material far more swiftly? However we answer these questions, there would seem to be a widespread belief that there's not enough political satire in this country. The *Wharf Revue* has tried to answer that particular call.

In its short history the *Wharf Revue* has charted the contraction of the democratic tradition of parliamentary debate in this country. It has been the response of one team of writer-performers to an increasingly vociferous audience demand for an oppositional viewpoint to the monolith of the party-political system. The Federal Government's introduction in late 2005 of anti-terrorism legislation, which included reinvigorated sedition laws, provoked an angry reaction from a wide coalition of civil libertarians, authors, publishers, artists and performers, who saw the laws as a threat to free speech.

For a brief, frightening period, the right of the theatre to speak freely about issues of social and political importance was directly challenged. It was only after an intense campaign by this wide coalition that amendments to the proposed laws were made. Even then, the laws retained worrying implications for the writers and performers of satire. Furthermore, for us, as for other artists who work within a subsidised-company structure, does there not still remain an implicit threat of self-censorship? Are not the major theatre companies, or public broadcasters like the ABC and SBS, likely to think twice before presenting material that might fall within the ambit of the sedition laws, or at best provoke lengthy and costly legal action?

The amended statutes have been the subject of a review by the Australian Law Reform Commission and their initial discussion paper, which was released in late May 2006, proposed some changes. However, even if all the recommended changes are implemented by the Attorney-General—and there is no certainty of that, of course—the freedom of artists to argue contentious, oppositional points of view remains under threat. Central to the proposed changes is the introduction of a contextual defence: when considering charges of incitement to violence, the jury should be asked to consider whether the alleged criminal acts were perpetrated as, or during the performance of, a work of art.

But how are we to define a work of art? Is it likely that a consensus of definition, something that has challenged expert minds for at least a century and a half, will be quickly reached by a jury of 'ordinary citizens'? As has been demonstrated so many times in the past, the definition of what constitutes artistic merit or integrity is subjective at best. And it is likely to be all the more so in the current climate of suspicion and fear, the very climate that demands healthy political satire.

The tradition we inherited

What, exactly, is revue? It has similarities to cabaret, vaudeville, variety and music hall, but, for our purposes, we can safely say that it is a collection of songs, sketches and comic pieces reflecting on topical themes, often of a socio-political or satirical nature. Parody and lampooning are a great Australian pastime that has thrived from the colony's earliest years, particularly in the pantomimes of journalists-turned-playwrights like W.M. Akhurst and Marcus Clarke from the 1860s in the lead-up to Federation. The style was taken up by the *Bulletin*. The revue tradition that we generally recognise in this country today grew out of the West End revues of the early twentieth century, which in their turn grew out of vaudeville and the music hall and, to a lesser extent, European cabaret of the previous century. By 1900, university revue societies already had a substantial history—the Cambridge Footlights first performed in 1883—but these student troupes rarely ventured onto the commercial stage.

Revue was the sophisticated alternative to the more working-class music-hall or variety bill; an evening sorbet of sketches, comic monologues, songs and musical items of vaguely topical interest that parodied or satirised the fashions and fads of the day, all supported by elaborate sets, costumes and an equally elaborate *corps de ballet*. Intimate revue was devised in reaction to the staggering cost of elaborate sets, costumes and *corps de ballet* and focused instead on the talents of an ensemble of performers. The lower overheads allowed producers to play smaller theatres and gave the writers greater flexibility. While this enabled them to respond more quickly to current events, they rarely, if ever, alluded to politics.

Australian audiences, with a fondness for variety best expressed by the glory days of the Tivoli, were reintroduced to intimate revue in 1947, when a local version of the hit London show, *Sweetest and Lowest*, opened at the Minerva Theatre in Sydney. That show marked the beginning of a revival of revue, burlesque and music hall that thrived readily in NSW and other capitals. In Melbourne, revue largely transmogrified into the more favoured format of stand-up comedy—of which Rod Quantock is perhaps the most overtly political exponent—or the satirical character-monologue that characterises the work of Max Gillies and Barry Humphries. Certain aspects of revue were also celebrated, of course, in Graham Kennedy's long-running TV show, *In Melbourne Tonight*.

The foundations of Australia's most famous revue were laid in 1953, when William Orr opened *Metropolitan Merry-Go-Round* at the Metropolitan Theatre in Sydney's Pitt Street. The writers included John McKellar, Gerry Donovan and Lance Mulcahy, a trio that went on to form the core of the creative teams that produced revue shows for more than ten years at the legendary Phillip Street Theatre, born when Orr moved to the 300-seat St James Hall in Phillip Street the following year.

In 1955, Melburnians first witnessed the glorious horror of Barry Humphries' unstoppable creation, Edna Everage, in the Union Theatre Repertory Company's revue, *Return Fare*, and audiences north of the border nudged her along the road to fame and fortune in an otherwise forgettable show called *Mr and Mrs* the following year. By this time, when radio drama was the only real bread-and-butter option, the Phillip Street revues were providing consistent employment for actors and writers. Many performers who went on to become household names got their break in revue—Ruth Cracknell, Reg Livermore, June Salter, Gordon Chater, Wendy Blacklock, Judi Farr, Robina Beard and Jill Perryman. Writers like Peter

Kenna, well before he crafted his classic *A Hard God*, churned out sketch material, and even the eminent Peter Sculthorpe composed the occasional piece for Phillip Street's two pit pianos.

But the Phillip Street fare was essentially social satire: the sketches drew on topical events, but steered clear of political life. Parodies of J.C. Williamson musicals and their ubiquitous leading lady, Evie Hayes; or of a pair of snobbish Market Street shop walkers; detergent manufacturers' slogans set to operatic arias, or Pierre of Balmain, featuring Gordon Chater as a highly camp couturier. Sketches such as these, based on immediately recognisable aspects of the Australian and, more particularly, the Sydney character, were the order of the day.

In 1961, the company moved to bigger premises in Elizabeth Street, renamed the Phillip Theatre, and Orr revamped the format by reducing his cast sizes, by limiting his sets to one basic unit and, importantly, by sharpening the satirical content of the scripts. These developments were in part inspired by the work of Britain's Peter Cook, Dudley Moore, Jonathan Miller and Alan Bennett, whose seminal *Beyond the Fringe* set a new benchmark in satirical writing and performance. That benchmark was raised after 1968, when the Lord Chamberlain's discretionary powers of censorship were abolished, permitting unrestrained lampooning of current political figures.[1]

The year 1964 was particularly significant, for it was then that revue was taken up by the relatively new medium of television, with Gordon Chater, Carol Raye and Barry Creyton banding together on *The Mavis Bramston Show*. Its tight turnarounds of weekly production enabled television to achieve a far greater immediacy, and the Phillip Street box-office took a beating. If the stage retaliated, it was largely due to the individual brilliance of John McKellar and his uncanny ability to encapsulate the Australian character. Some of his best lines, like 'A cup of tea, a Bex and a good lie-down', quickly entered the vernacular. Theatre had one other advantage; it didn't consume material at the furnace-like rate of television. And the theatre continued its long tradition of fostering talent. Perhaps the most outstanding example was the Architecture Revue at the University of Sydney, which in its forma-tive years in the mid-1960s, boasted the talents of Grahame Bond, Rory O'Donoghue, Peter Weir and Geoffrey Atherden, all of whom went on to substantial careers in the film and television industries.

Then 1984 saw a brief flickering revival of stage revue with the John McKellar retrospective, *Four Lady Bowlers in a Golden Holden*, at Kinsela's in Sydney. Kinsela's also ran the more politically charged *Balmain Boys Don't Cry* before fading away once more. Out of Nimrod Downstairs came Tony Sheldon and Tony Taylor's hugely popular *You and the Night and the House Wine* (1980) and in other venues, revue shows would spasmodically surface, none of them overtly political, preferring instead to focus on the traditional social satire of the Phillip Street genre. But then in 1981 Max Gillies opened his first satirical revue, *Squirts*, in Adelaide, then Melbourne, in which he played 17 characters, including Prime Ministers Menzies and Fraser. This was followed by *A Night with the Right* (1983) and, for ABC-TV, *The Gillies Report* (1984).

7

Whereas stage revue had tended to avoid political subject matter, preferring to target social mores and the curious demands of fashion, television was again able to take the song-and-dance traditions of the stage and give them a political edge. Gillies, along with writers John Clarke and Patrick Cook and under the watchful eye of director Ted Robinson, created seminal programmes. *The Late Show* and *The D-Generation* made the successful transition from the university revue stage to the small television screen, and in 1987 I got my own first taste of putting across political satire, as a writer-actor in *The Dingo Principle* for ABC-TV. Our popular and critical reception was on the underside of whelming, although we did manage to get a few Australian diplomats expelled from the Middle East and provoke angry words from the Soviet ambassador.

There are a few surviving television political satires: having begun by producing a fortnightly satirical newspaper, *The Chaser* team went on to front a number of series for ABC-TV, and on the same network *The Glasshouse* combines the stand-up tradition with political and social commentary. Interestingly, *The Chaser* team have also dabbled in live stage revue with some success. But, on the whole, television, particularly the public broadcaster, has felt the constraints of production costs and political pressure. I have it on good authority that a senior ABC policy executive actually asked if it might be possible to have more even-handed satire, and if the satirical duo of John Clark and Brian Dawe could target someone other the Howard Government a little more often. Fortunately, to this point, the stage has not been subjected to the same editorial pressures. Theatre's traditional freedom to lampoon our masters in an open public forum, a freedom enjoyed since the ancient days of Aristophanes, remains largely intact.

Why bring revue back?

The *Wharf Revue* began its life in 2000, when Robyn Nevin, the recently appointed artistic director of the Sydney Theatre Company (STC), fulfilled a long-standing ambition to initiate an ongoing revue stream within the company's operations. A fan of revue ever since the glory days of Phillip Street, where she had seen a number of shows, she had tried in 1984 to persuade former director Richard Wherrett to include political satire in the STC's programme. But discussions got nowhere: Wherrett favoured cabaret and music theatre. When she herself took over, Nevin says, she had a vision of the revue, as a 'snapshot of contemporary Australia. A visitor could land in Sydney, come down to the *Wharf Revue* and get an immediate sense of political life at the time.'

Coupled with her personal liking for the genre, Nevin was also confronted by a dearth of main-stage writing that dealt with topical political issues. Contemporary playwrights like David Williamson were more interested in social and gender politics and, *Don's Party* or *The Great Man* aside, he tended to steer clear of direct comment on politics at a federal or state level. In Nevin's opinion, the STC had no tradition of political drama: no political writing had been commissioned by the company.

With one exception: at the time of Nevin's accession, the company had an existing commission with Stephen Sewell, arguably Australia's most politically charged playwright. That commission had been unfulfilled, so Nevin and her artistic associate Stephen Armstrong steered it into a collaborative work with the Flying Fruit Fly Circus. (The project went through a creative workshop and draft design process, but never progressed to a full production due to inadequate financial support.) Since that time, no major work of Sewell's has been performed by the STC, something which, given his public outbursts against Nevin and the subsidised state companies in general, appears still to rankle. The only writing Sewell has done for the STC stage has been a sketch that we included in our 2000 revue, *The Unofficial Visitors' Guide to Australia*, about the police shooting of Ron Levi on Bondi Beach in 1997.

That issue aside, Armstrong felt that the little political writing the STC did receive was judged to be insufficiently theatrical—too didactic and bordering on the diatribe. He also surmised that an 'innate fear of unresolved tension and a wish to offer some sort of hope at a play's conclusion' prevented dramatists from being able to reflect political realities. The unavoidable fact is that a full-length mainstage production's need for a substantial period of gestation, preparation and rehearsal makes instantaneous response to political events virtually impossible. By the time David Hare's political drama, *Stuff Happens*, for example, about the politics leading up to the war in Iraq, reached the Sydney stage in July 2005—ten months after it had opened in London—it was somewhat yesterday's newspaper. In order to give it some local immediacy, Company B Belvoir arranged for a reference to Australia's participation in the Coalition of the Willing to be inserted.

Robyn Nevin believed that a satirical revue could fill the gap and respond to an audience that she knew existed for what she called 'an opposing voice'. However, given her responsibilities to subsidising other streams of programming, the decision was made to not underwrite the new venture: it had to stand or fall on its own commercial merits. Nevin's initial concern was that it should 'succeed as entertainment'. Thereafter she would give 'gentle encouragement to moving it toward being more political'.

Rob Brookman, the STC's general manager, has acknowledged that the commercial risk was minimal and after six years of the experiment, he's been 'pleasantly surprised by the results'. After initially playing late-night time slots in Wharf 1 on the pre-existing mainstage production's set, the revue established itself more quickly than anticipated and, in response to audience demand, moved to a designated theatre (Wharf 2). Expected to attract a younger audience, it was in fact embraced by a demographic that all but matched that of the company's subscriber base. Not that the perceived conservatism of the subscribers to a subsidised theatre company was likely to prove an obstacle, in Brookman's view. A 'satire audience is able to separate [its] political allegiances,' he thought—and over the years his view has been confirmed by critical reactions. As one reviewer has since written, 'It would take a pretty staunch pro-Liberal not to crack a smile at the antics of the *Revue* cast.'[2]

Revue audiences, whatever their political persuasion, take comfort from having their prejudices confirmed. Stephen Armstrong calls it the genre's 'capacity to reference immediately what you know. You feel informed, not stupid, as you watch it. Not needing to conform to rigid dramatic structures, the placement of the material can explode the way it is received—you're drawn in, then slapped in the face.' Revue, Nevin believes, is 'a licence to say things that serious artists cannot'. It's a dramatic form that, by definition, takes risks, and that, for Armstrong, is a good thing: 'Community standards are determined by the level of risk taken by artists—you discover community standards when you go to the revue.'

Geez—and I always thought we were doing it for the laughs!

A short history of the *Wharf Revue*: From cheap laughs to seditious intent

I n fact, at the beginning we *were* only 'doing it for the laughs'. That's not to say that there was no underlying serious purpose, simply that the accent was placed firmly on light-hearted fun. As I look back today over the six years that the *Wharf*

Revue has been running—does that make us one of Australia's longest-running ensemble companies?—I can see a steady progression towards purely political satire. We even reached a point in 2005 where we were prepared to forgo laughs for more than the statutory minute! In the pages that follow I want to chart this development and consider why and how the revue has responded to a growing demand for an oppositional political voice.

2000, February–March:
The End of the Wharf as We Know It[3]

> We are going legit at the end of the Wharf.
> We are raising our standards because we are
>   funded.
> We used to make jokes about arses and wear funny
>   glasses
> And feeble disguises and give away prizes.
> Now we're honing our wit
> And we're tastefully lit.
> You want Art? This is it!
> At the end of the Wharf—we are going legit!

After several years of modest success with a series of cabaret/revue shows that went under the banner of *Three Men and a Baby Grand*, we—that is, long-time colleagues Drew Forsythe and Phil Scott, and myself, and with the help of Linda Nagle—decided to attempt something a little more ambitious for the millennium year 2000 (or 2001, depending on your level of pedantry). It was to be a revue that provided a snapshot of the nation as we approached what seemed to be a turning point. We approached Wayne

Harrison, the STC's artistic director at the time, and, somewhat to our surprise—he shared his precedessor's liking for cabaret and music theatre—he liked the idea and promptly commissioned the show. With our typical showbiz fortune, however, Wayne left his position shortly afterwards, so our 'millennium show script' lay forgotten in the bottom of a filing cabinet, along with early *Tap Dogs* fliers and polite but firm rejection notices for aspiring playwrights.

Being keen advocates of recycling, however, when Robyn Nevin commissioned us to produce our first revue, we were quick to revive material from the abandoned show as the basis of the script. Sketches included the first meeting of the organising committee of the ancient games of the Olympiad; a new tourism campaign for Lord Howe Island, led by colourful resident, Ned Dignam; the 999 millennium show; an episode of *Playschool*, directed by Neil Armfield and Barrie Kosky, and a mini-opera about the controversial redevelopment of Walsh Bay in Sydney.

It was this last item that provoked our first test of editorial independence. We had written the piece with the help of research from Geraldine O'Brien, heritage writer for the *Sydney Morning Herald*. The then chairman of the STC's board of directors had strongly promoted the idea of the company's place within the newly developed Walsh Bay precinct. Indeed, largely through his influence with one of the project's developers, he had been instrumental in securing a new 800-seat theatre for the STC as an integral part of the development application. There was concern within STC management that the Walsh Bay sketch, which questioned the motives and heritage values of the development, might prove an embarrassment to the board and, in particular, to its chairman. Board member Henric Nicholas QC, a specialist in defamation and media law, was brought in to advise on the legal implications of the sketch. He recommended the alteration of a few words, and gave it the all clear. Then, once they had seen a rehearsal of the material that had raised concerns, the other directors acknowledged that artistic interference from board level was inappropriate, and the sketch was allowed to go ahead.

The End of the Wharf as We Know It also saw the introduction of Walt Disney (no relation), the multi-purpose New Zealand bureaucrat, who gave an address about the tax implications of the recently introduced Goods and Services Tax—for the sex industry. Aside from the Walsh Bay sketch, this was the only item in the show with political implications.

2000, August–September:
The Unofficial Visitors' Guide to Australia

CHARLIE: [*dying*] I love you, Peter Lalor,
    For you I took a bullet.
    You want to know the real me?
    Just grab my plait and pull it.
    You called me names, rejected me—
    I wasn't European.
    Ironically, I'm not Chinese.
    In fact, I'm South Korean!
    Me go now.

CHARLIE *dies and a distraught* LALOR *kisses her lifeless form.*

LALOR: Korea! I just kissed a girl from Korea!

> From the finale, *Eureka! The Musical*
> (Not the real one, which didn't reach the
> stage until 2004.)

In the hysteria leading up to Sydney's hosting of the Olympic Games in September 2000, the second revue turned the spotlight on Australiana, in order to familiarise our visitors with local social mores and customs. Records remain unclear as to how many visitors actually attended, but the show was given the Wharf 2 theatre. Items included a commission from David Williamson, the Reduced Williamson Company performing the beginning, middle and end of each (well, quite a few) of his plays in under five minutes; a memorable appearance by Jacki Weaver, dressed as a depressed marsupial, singing the haunting 'Koala from Sofala'; the bush ballad of Shanghai Neville, failed bushranger; two CWA ladies running through the culinary delights of the Association's cookbook; and a mini-musical based on the Eureka Stockade uprising and revolving around the unrequited love of a Korean immigrant goldminer (disguised) for rebellion leader, Peter Lalor.

The programme also included two pieces of vaguely political satire: a Jacobean verse tragedy about the rivalry between the Packer and Murdoch dynasties, and a solo performance by Drew Forsythe as TV gardening guru, Peter Cundall, examining plants of the *genus parliamentaria* held in the national collection in Canberra. This was our first concerted effort at massaging political content into accessible parodic form.

The threat of censorship was again raised, this time over a sketch featuring Jason Sponge, a young interpretative jazz-ballet artiste and member of the Young Nationals, who was attempting to counter the perception of the National Party as a racist organisation by performing a dance of Indigenous reconciliation at their annual conference. The irony of using a medley of Rolf Harris's 'Sun Arise', Charlie Drake's 'My Boomerang Won't Come Back' and Yothu Yindi's 'Treaty' as a genuine attempt to bridge the cultural divide seemed to escape the young dancer. It certainly escaped elements of STC management, who deemed the sketch to be borderline offensive. Of particular concern to them was the fact that the revue would be sharing Wharf 2 with a troupe of Indigenous actors performing *Black Medea* under the direction of Wesley Enoch. Cultural sensitivity—or political correctness, then at the height of its considerable powers—won out: the sketch was dropped before it was publicly performed. All to the bemusement of Wesley Enoch, who long after the event told me that he'd used Charlie Drake's timely parable about incompetent boomerang-throwing on stage many times, to great comic effect.

2000, November–December:
Beyond Our Control

Beyond Our Control saw the reunion of three of the original stars of *You and the Night and the House Wine*, Tony Sheldon, Tony Taylor and Robyn Moase, to write and perform what was very much a return to the Phillip Street style of intimate revue, i.e. devoid of any material that could be considered political. Opening with a celebration of the return to some sort of normality after the Olympic juggernaut had left town, the running order included a tribute to light rail, the Aussie invasion of Hollywood, Luddites, Chopper Read, group therapy, the computer age and synchronised swimming live on stage.

The show also included what has been for me one of the funniest *Wharf Revue* sketches to date. In a John McKellar-esque moment of theatrical absurdity, Tony Taylor sang 'Gigi', while Tony Sheldon provided an offstage series of two-packs-a-day responses as the bronchially-challenged object of the singer's affections. It was pure revue: a simple idea brilliantly performed, a sentimental piece of nostalgia sweetly arranged and sung as the rug was ripped from beneath its feet with hysterical results.

2001, March–April:
Free Petrol

As an election year and the centenary of Federation, 2001 inspired us to move somewhat more purposefully down the political path. From the opening number—about the lengths to which political parties will go in order to ensure voter support—the bulk of the material was political: a committee meeting of the policy advisers who really run the country; neo-conservatism in rural electorates; Alan and Grant, two stalwart supporters of the Democrats, throwing a party to which no one else turns up; the CWA ladies presenting the history of Federation by means of a cake diorama; the recently deposed Democrats' leader, Meg Lees, singing a ballad of regret; and, as the finale, a mini-musical in the style of *Guys and Dolls* about Sydney Lord Mayor Frank Sartor and his proposed electoral boundary changes.

We took the opportunity to demonstrate what revue can do best, namely respond quickly to political events that strike an absurdist note. The electoral routing of the Queensland Liberal Party at the state poll was one such event. The Liberals were left with just three sitting members, so—how might a leadership challenge play out in the party room?

> *The parliamentary office of the Queensland Liberals. Three desks with telephones, the front desk has two.* JON *is addressing the troops.*

JON: So, in conclusion, let's remember, there might only be three of us, but we are the Queensland Parliamentary Liberal Party and we have to stay tight, focused and start winning the next election.

> *Polite applause and all three go to their desks. A phone rings.*

Hello? You're from where? The *Courier Mail?* And you've heard rumours of a leadership challenge? That's a load of rubbish. Look, mate, I can tell you, as parliamentary leader, I know I have the full and unhesitating support of my two colleagues ...

> VALERIE *and* DREW *have been listening intently, but, as* JON *pauses, they quickly lower their heads.*

Er ... can I call you back?

JON looks worried and takes a suspicious look at VALERIE *and* DREW *who busy themselves at their desks.* JON *dials a number. Phone rings, and* DREW *picks it up.*

Drew, mate? Jon here. Look, have you heard anything about a leadership challenge?

DREW: Nothing to do with me, mate.

JON: So I have your continued support?

DREW: Jon. Mate. At the end of the day, as your deputy leader, I give you ...

JON: But you're not my deputy leader.

DREW: Eh?

JON: Valerie's the deputy. I gave you Shadow Veterans' Affairs and National Parks.

DREW: Really? Since when?

JON: Since the Chinese dinner we had last Thursday.

DREW: Oh.

JON: So do I have your support?

DREW: Er ... can I ring you back on this?

JON: Yeah, no worries, mate.

Both hang up. DREW *looks around furtively, then dials a number. Phone rings.* VALERIE *answers it.*

VALERIE: Hello?

DREW: Valerie? Drew, Veterans' Affairs and National Parks. Look, have you heard anything about a leadership challenge?

VALERIE: Should I have?

DREW: Jon just rang me asking for support.

VALERIE: What are you suggesting?

DREW: Maybe it's time for a woman in the top job.

VALERIE: And what's in it for you? Deputy?

DREW: Well, I'm pretty busy with Veterans' Affairs and National Parks. Very happy here. But, look, in this game you learn to never say 'never'.

VALERIE: Have you got the numbers?

DREW: What say I work the phones, crunch the figures and get back to you?

VALERIE: OK.

> *They hang up.* DREW *thinks, then dials a number. Phone rings, and* VALERIE *answers.*

DREW: It's Drew.

VALERIE: That was quick.

DREW: Just ringing to see if you're on side for a leadership challenge. We put Valerie in the top job.

VALERIE: This is Valerie.

DREW: So I can count you in?

VALERIE: Of course you can.

DREW: Brilliant. Oh, and keep it quiet.

> *They hang up,* VALERIE *in some confusion.* DREW *talks to himself.*

OK, that's two.

> *He dials a number. Phone rings.*

JON: Hello?

DREW: Drew, Affairs and Parks. Just ringing to see if you're on side for a leadership challenge.

JON: I am the leader!

DREW: Er … solly, long number. Me go now.

JON *dials a number. Phone rings.*

VALERIE: Hello?

JON: Do you know anything about this leadership challenge?

VALERIE: I'm sorry, Jon, I tried to keep a lid on it but the backbench are getting nervous …

JON: We haven't got a backbench! We can hold a cabinet meeting in a phone box, for Christ's sake!

VALERIE: Look, I know you're hurting right now, but this is no reflection on your leadership, it's simply a matter of reading the public mood.

JON: We've got three seats, Valerie—Helen Keller could read the public mood with her hands tied behind her back!

VALERIE: I don't think jokes about the physically challenged are going to help in this very difficult transitional period.

JON: Well, maybe I could be your deputy?

VALERIE: Have you got the numbers?

JON: What are you talking about? We've got two votes to one!

VALERIE: That's not a convincing win. Sends a very mixed signal to the business community.

DREW *dials a number.*

Can you hold, Jon? I've got call waiting. Hello?

DREW: We've got two. Might be enough to swing it.

VALERIE: Jon wants to be deputy.

DREW: You said I could.

VALERIE: But I can get his car space—it's nearer the lift than yours.

DREW: Jon had his chance. He's finished!

JON: I can hear you!

DREW: [*whispering into the phone*] I'll give you two cab-charge vouchers a week.

VALERIE: Four.

Exasperated, JON *slams the phone down and stands up to speak to the others.*

JON: This is bloody childish! Why don't we decide the issue the same way we did last time, like sane, rational adults?

VALERIE: Alright.

DREW: Fair enough.

JON *sits down and puts his head in his arms.* VALERIE *and* DREW *look around, then scarper.*

JON: Two … four … six … eight … ten! Coming, ready or not!

Free Petrol toured to the Adelaide Cabaret Festival and it was there that we received the first threat of a defamation suit. In a sketch based on the TV show *The Weakest Link,* featuring Peter Costello, Peter Reith and Tony Abbott as contestants, a reference was made to a prominent conservative media figure working for News Limited in Sydney. In deference to local sensibilities, we substituted South Australia's conservative publisher and former Liberal Party speechwriter, Christopher Pearson. Pearson was informed by a friend of his inclusion and, despite the fact that he never actually saw the offending material himself, promptly fired off a solicitor's letter warning us of dire consequences if the reference to him was not immediately withdrawn.

Initially, the revue scripts were all vetted by the STC's lawyers. They agreed that Pearson had a weak case, but, with typical legal equivocation, could not guarantee an eventual outcome in our favour. After consultation with Rob Brookman, we decided the reference was not worth the trouble or expense of defending a suit, so we dropped it. It was no great loss: it had fast become obvious that Christopher Pearson was known to rather fewer people than we had imagined, let alone thought by them to be an object of amusement.

When the revue returned to Sydney, we reinstated our original target, the feisty News Limited columnist Piers Akerman. No doubt alerted by his interstate ideological ally, he too had his solicitors fire off a stern letter demanding damages—even though he too had never seen the offending sketch. Again, we dropped the reference: no point in making a cheap joke prohibitively expensive. Incidentally, Mr Akerman came and enjoyed a later revue at the Wharf—so much so that he was last seen urinating into the Harbour!

2001, August–September:
Free Petrol, Too!

Free Petrol, Too! was the previous show coming back for a return season, but with new material added in order to give it more political bite. We now had Alexander Downer making a fool of himself at a CHOGM cocktail party by assuming the Indian Ambassador was simply there to serve the samosas, a relatively trivial misdemeanour compared with his failing to notice a $300 million wheat bribery scandal. (Ah, what innocent times they were back then!) The committee meeting sketch was rewritten to feature the advertising agency running the Federal Government's public information campaigns, widely regarded as taxpayer-funded election advertising. Democrats Alan and Grant took to the How-to-Vote booths with dispiriting results. And the few remaining True Believers held an Arts for Labor Launch, which included Bob Ellis, Roger and Bevan (two failed Opera Australia chorus gentlemen trying to reinvent themselves by becoming politically active) and aspiring cabaret chanteuse Geraldine Lemon-Lamond, who would perform at the opening of a fridge. She sang the following impassioned plea for the ALP:

Tonight I'm here with the cream of the industry,
The Arts—with a capital A for Apathy.
O for the days of 10BA,
Radio drama, the three-act play,
Australian stories on the screen.

Who cares who won the Tri-Nations Tiddlywinks,
Or what Dawn Fraser or Fatty Vautin thinks?
I wouldn't piss in the Bledisloe Cup!
We're so dumbed down now dumb is up!
We need more culture on the scene
And arty types like Simon Crean.

Eight years ago you won a Keating,
Now eight per cent of us are eating.
There was a time when we came through for
    Gough,
Then Fraser came along and blew us off.

Tonight we're here in support of the ALP.
That's right, it's time to sing for our subsidy.
So we'll lobby the House of Reps
With Fat Cat, Bert and Henri Szeps—
He's not a dentist, by the way.

It's time community clowns got work again.
It's time they saw *The Wild Duck* in Bourke again,
Living statues, white-faced mime,
The Seventeenth Doll for the eighteenth time.
It's now a case of do or die,
Or you can kiss your bleeding arts goodbye!

The whole tawdry affair was hosted by a disgruntled Judy Davis, played with uncanny accuracy by Valerie Bader. We ran into trouble when Ms Davis became aware of the piece, having read a review in the *Sydney Morning Herald*. Again, not having seen a performance, she instructed her agent to issue the strongest possible complaint. A number of factors prompted this. First, she had directed the STC production of *The School for Scandal*, which was playing in the Opera House at the time, and felt the company was betraying one of its own. She had also washed her hands of the ALP and resented any connection by association. (Incidentally, by contrast, Bob Ellis enjoyed seeing himself parodied so much that he saw the show five times.) Mediation via Davis's agent went nowhere and, although no explicit directive was issued by the STC management, pressure from somewhere was brought to bear on us to replace the item. Discretion being the better part of valour, we substituted Robyn Nevin (also played by Valerie Bader)—we even tried it with Bryan Brown!—but the sketch never worked as well.

It's ironic that to date the only threats against political items in the revue have been made by figures from the arts and media establishment. When are we going to be sued by a politician?

2002, March–April:
The Year of Living Comfortably

In the wake of John Howard's 2001 *Tampa*-led election victory, it was inevitable that the mini-musical finale—already established as something of a tradition—should be about border protection and the vexed question of asylum seekers. Perhaps it's no less inevitable that in 2006, as I sit writing this, it is proposed that the entire continental mass of Australia be excluded from the migration zone and all 'illicit' boat arrivals ordered to be processed offshore. *South Pacific Solution* opened with ...

> *A boat in swirling fog, filled with asylum seekers.*

ASSORTED BOATPERSONS:
> From a nation divided, a people oppressed,
> We seek a new life in the welcoming West.
> With only the clothes on my back,
> And my mother-in-law in a sack,
> A goat and two pigs, a packet of figs,
> A Danielle Steele to read on the boat ...
> Can't wait to vote!
> We've spent our life savings, we're huddling,
>   poor and distressed.
>
> I have a cousin who lives in Lakemba.
> I had nothing to do with the tragic events of
>   September.

Neither did we!

We've been promised a unit in Rushcutters Bay,
Five hundred dollars and no more to pay.
I'm a surgeon, I've got a degree,
But my daughter can't count up to three.
I'll work like a slave. Please let me shave!
For Mohammed el Howard I'll lay down my
     life—and his wife!
Our troubles are over; we set course for freedom
     today!

Australia calls, we hasten to her shore,
Sweet land of barbecues galore.
We've seen the brochure—it all looks kosher
Soon we won't be drinking urine any more!

Later, after the boat has landed:

We paid to come to a special island!
A wide brown land that is girt by sea!

MINISTER: But you'll be sent to another island,
So we can exploit this opportunity ...
On Nauru, you'll be processed,
Like the fish John West rejects.
You will sleep in concrete hammocks,
Grouped by age, weight and sex.

On Nauru, you'll be forgotten,
Out of sight, out of mind,
In a land made out of guano
From a seagull's behind.

On Nauru, if you're unhappy,
You can call the UN.
We'll install a working phone line
In 2010.

Buoyed by their unexpected electoral success, the
Coalition shifted the political agenda further to

the right and tightened their control on both the parliament and internal party discipline. If anything, this fuelled our determination to include more political material.

Tony Abbott, self-appointed head-kicker of the day and Leader of Government Business in the House, became a target himself in the Monsieur Thenardier-inspired song 'Master of the House'. Quiet revenge was taken upon Mr Akerman in the form of Drew Forsythe's bloated Bile Man, a foaming right-wing columnist, waging a one-man culture war, while globalisation and the free market were all but undone by the stinging attacks on product placement in the Taco Bell Shakespeare Company and the world domination by Starbucks. The staff of Radio National, forced underground by Communications Minister Richard Alston as he waged an intense personal war on the ABC, were forced to perform *The Goons* live to air, after Robert Dessaix accidentally sat on the recordings. *The Goon Show* in question dealt with the vexed issue of the economic sustainability of a third domestic airline—not a subject that traditionally screams laughter, but, believe me, given the right context and some excellent Bloodnok fart jokes, comic life can be breathed into even the driest political issue!

The show also included a sketch about Barry Jones and a few other recovering socialists attending a self-help group and embarking on a twelve-step programme, in order to rid themselves of lingering left-wing tendencies and enable them to take their places as responsible members of the ALP.

It is not the job of revue to have favourites, but

to satirise politics of all persuasions. This 'take no prisoners' approach strengthens the validity of our criticisms, which become more difficult to dismiss as party-political grandstanding. On the other hand, it's hardly surprising that, in this decade of sustained right-wing government, the conservatives should find themselves more often on the receiving end than any other party. Whatever our personal political allegiances as writers—and we make no secret of these—this is not a case of inherent bias, rather of unavoidable bias, given that the intrinsic role of satire is to specifically target those who actually wield the power and influence.

However, there are those who believe that an ideological position is imperative. Rod Quantock, for example, veteran of the political stand-up comedy scene—he practically *is* that scene!—has difficulty in offending the ALP. As he said on ABC radio in the early years of the Howard Government:

> I think there's a group of comedians who would be politically non-aligned, apathetic even. I mean to the point where there's a very popular view that all politicians are stupid, which is very helpful to politicians because you've dismissed them out of hand [... s]o there is a range of comedians [who] don't look very carefully at the issues [...].[4]

Such blanket public cynicism is exacerbated in this age of an emasculated Opposition that is choked of oxygen by the bypassing of traditional parliamentary debate, Senate accountability and a tightly controlled Government media agenda.

Indeed, the tighter the Government's control of the national agenda becomes, and the more successfully John Howard exploits what has been described as 'democratic majoritarianism' by marginalising any opposition, the more vital satire becomes to our national well-being. It is Robyn Nevin's contention that the *Wharf Revue* 'provid[es] a service to the community, offering an oppositional viewpoint and a release from the frustration of a lack of engagement between the political process and the community'. And Rob Brookman echoes this sentiment: 'As the Government's media control and increasingly clever tactics stifle debate, the [*Wharf Revue*] provides points of resistance that can only be to the good. [It is] for people who feel battered by their impotence in the face of the monolith the Government has become, providing a sense of "I'm not alone".'

The phenomenon is not confined to Australia. The Italian elections this year were fought in extraordinary circumstances, namely that the lion's share of the country's mass media was under the family control of the incumbent leader, Prime Minister Silvio Berlusconi. Political satirists became one of the few sources of an alternative viewpoint, not only on television but also in live performance, echoing the South African experience under apartheid, in which the theatre offered one of the few points of resistance.

2002, November–December:
Much Revue About Nothing

Barry Jones returned to address the annual conference of the ALP and try to explain the party's factional system in the same way as he had previously presented Knowledge Nation. In the real world, this was a policy initiative immediately derided by the Government wits as 'Noodle Nation'—an abject lesson in the power of simple words and mockery; the policy was effectively killed by laughing at Jones's impenetrably complicated graphic representation of it.

Democrats Alan and Grant used the inter-parliamentary netball play-offs as a colourful analogy to the party's leadership merry-go-round, while the confessional box became the latest hunting ground for the legal profession, with lawyers prepared to act on behalf of both priest and penitent. Leadership aspirant Mark Latham also made his first appearance, trading insults with Drew Forsythe's frightening impression of Michelle Grattan—to our great discomfort when, at one Sunday matinee, the real Michelle Grattan was spotted in the second row!

In late 2002, the seeds were being busily sown for the Iraq War II, an ongoing theme that has fuelled us now for four years. The mini-musical finale was based on the startling concept of Foreign Minister Alexander Downer being smuggled into Iraq to pre-empt a proposed US pre-emptive strike …

> DOWNER: Ooh, I shall have to assume a secret
> identity. An undercover name … Let me see …
> I know, Alexander Doona! A 30-million-dollar
> killing machine owned by the Government. If
> only I had one.
>
> *Sings.*
>
> I've been given a vital mission;
> Never had a mission before!
> My code name is Alexander;
> I'm busting to go to war.

Armed with nothing but skill and cunning
And depending on where I land,
I'll fight the foreign foe,
Hope I don't stub my toe
On the line drawn in the sand.
I'm Alexander's One-Man Band!

> *Speaks.*

Ooh, better check my equipment.

> *Sings again.*

A three-man tent with annexe,
Multiple-use sarong,
Gentian Violet and bandage,
Fifty metres long,
Army knife and compass,
Shoes with animal prints,
A fully inflatable rubber canoe,
And some after-dinner mints.

A ten-day pass on Eurail,
Commencing a week ago (damn!),
A wig and a pair of fishnets,
In case we put on a show.
A shapeless piece of rubber,
The Michelin Guide to Iraq,
Retractable pegless clothesline
And a Kelloggs' Variety Pack.

So I'm set for my big adventure.
Evil tyrants can never win.
Saddam will feel the blade
Of the Wolf of Adelaide!
Let the Holy War begin!
Alexander's going in!

Despite assistance from two ASIO operatives disguised as a camel and a helpful arms-dealer in Basra,

Alexander failed almost immediately. Commander-in-Chief Howard decided to send in their best agent to get him back. And so Amanda Vanstone was dropped from a great height into the desert. After discovering a strange love for one another beneath the desert stars, Vanstone and Downer were quickly arrested and brought before Saddam. Funnily enough, the trio also quickly discovered a mutual respect for strong, centralised government, old-fashioned family values and a 'get tough on crime' attitude. Sadly, however, they all met an untimely end from a pre-emptive bunker buster.

I believe that the Iraqi Musical constitutes our most satisfying attempt yet to be the theatrical equivalent of the political cartoon. Australia has a long tradition of political cartooning that stretches back to the early years of the colony, and the capacity of the satirical black-and-white drawing to articulate succinctly the follies and shortcomings of the political system makes it for many the most potent feature of the print media. Cartoonists have a licence to say things that are given to no other journalist or commentator. The theatre can enjoy the same freedoms: thinly disguised as a joke, political revue can assume the role of the court-appointed Fool, telling those who listen how closely farce and tragedy sit together. And looking back at the eventual conduct of the war in the Middle East, our Iraqi Musical seems only marginally less farcical than what we're shown on the nightly news bulletins.

The elder statesman of Australian cartooning, Bruce Petty, fears that the court has eclipsed its Fools—that reality is outstripping imagination and threatening to leave satirists behind actual events.[5] In my view, revue is perfectly capable of meeting that challenge, allowing, as it does, the juxtaposition of an enormous range of theatrical devices against the grim reality of current affairs, stripping away the pretensions of policy decisions and exposing their inherent absurdity.

2003, June–August:
Sunday in Iraq with George

One of the memorable features of the *Wharf Revue* has been the musical contribution of Phil Scott. A veteran of *The Gillies Report*, Phil composes music that can lend an extraordinarily emotive complexity to our material. The secret of satire, of all comedy, lies as much in the delivery as in the content, and music can give unpalatable material a relish, at least an accessibility, it might not otherwise have.

> Free Trade!
> We've got it made,
> If we can persuade
> The US of A
>
> To give way
> On Free Trade.
> Free Trade
> Cannot be delayed.
>
> When a country such as Australia has produced
> a lot of stuff
> Which we can't foist on someone else, then life
> can soon become real tough.
> But with Free Trade, we can offload each glut to
> end up in the black

On a market which will replace the one we lost
    in old Iraq.
Since the attack, we can't get it back.

Our beef and lamb are good and cheap.
They're much too good for us to keep.
And what about our chardonnay?
Let's marinate the USA!
We can do fuel, though not much oil,
But we do things that grow in soil.
What a killing we will make!
Americans eat prawns with steak!

Hell hath not a greater fury
Than a farmer in Missouri
When he finds the local shops
Are full of Aussie lamb neck chops.
Californian vignerons are
Gonna think it's not so bonza.
Sales are down and they are screamin'
On account of Peter Lehmann.

Let's be fair, we need to make a few concessions.
Don't despair, or weaken at the knees.
Qantas, Telstra, Channel 9 and all the papers
We will sell to buyers overseas.

The ABC will be alright
With *I Love Lucy* every night
And SBS will never vanish,
If it gets a bit more Spanish.
News on 7, 9 and 10
Already comes from CNN.
We'll put coyotes in our zoos,
We've had our fill of kangaroos!

But, hey now,
The USA now
Are saying they intend to keep their quotas

To appease their rural voters.
Free Trade?
Or me me me trade?
The level playing-field they recommend
Is only level at one end!

US protections stay in place as
We look on with smiling faces.
In the world of give-and-take the taker is the
    king.
Howard will be pleased as Punch,
The rest of us say, 'Thanks a bunch'.
Funny, but I have a hunch
Free Trade is like the old free lunch.
There's NO SUCH THING!

> From Phil Scott's solo number, 'Free Trade'

By now the *Wharf Revue* was well established and we were playing five nights a week, Wednesdays through Sundays. In this show, there was only one sketch that wasn't in some way political, a Sondheim-esque tribute to the Rolf Harris catalogue, parodying the modern juke-box musical. Elsewhere, Robert Brown of Launceston led his merry men of green in the Sherwood Olde Growth Forest; Senator Richard Alston had his own *Tonight* show on the ABC, and the last keepers of the Light on the Hill gathered for the funeral of the ALP. This sombre occasion degenerated into low farce, because the party's factional arrangements dictated six pallbearers on the right, but only one on the left! And then Gough embarrassed Margaret by throwing himself into the open grave, while Cheryl Kernot spat on the coffin.

Also on the running order was New Zealander Walt Disney, newly appointed Knowledge Consumer

Services Liaison Manager (formerly Vice-Chancellor) of the Baulkham Hills University (formerly Galston TAFE). His address to the undergraduates outlined their payment options and the Visa Awards Points bonuses available if they upsized their degrees.

The war in Iraq, we were told, was over—well, Baghdad had been captured, Saddam's statue pulled down and President Bush had declared the Mission Accomplished—so the musical was a Bing Crosby/Bob Hope road movie called *The Road to Damascus*, Syria being touted as next on the to-do list of the Coalition of the Willing. Bing and Bob were two Yankee carpet-baggers hunting down those elusive WMDs for sale to the highest bidder and had worked up a scam to pass off Australian food-aid parcels as chemical weapons. When things got a little too hot, they quickly set sail for the relative calm of North Korea.

2004, November–December:
Fast and Loose

Business as usual after yet another Coalition win: this time it was Mark Latham reading out the well-worn concession speech and a Government majority in the Senate in July 2005 being eagerly awaited on the Coalition benches. Due to our involvement with *The Republic of Myopia*, the musical that together with Katherine Thomson's *Harbour* opened the new Sydney Theatre in January 2004, there was only one *Wharf Revue* in 2004. It did, however, play the bigger Wharf 1 theatre for eight shows a week and continue the trend of providing a profit stream for the company. There was a darker edge to the script that reflected the writers' personal dissatisfaction with the state of the world, and material was selected on the basis of what provoked their anger as much as their laughter. We were soon to discover that it was a choice that very much reflected audience sentiment.

Max Gillies, the country's best-known political satirist, has witnessed a similar audience-driven demand for the shift to consistently topical, political material. His solo career began with a greater emphasis on socio-political, generic character types, but he feels he's been pushed—and not unwillingly—towards the portrayal of identifiable political figures and the policies they espouse. And certain figures readily lend themselves to lampooning. Pauline Hanson, who is only one of the more obvious, sang this ballad in *Fast and Loose*:

> I've been imprisoned and abused, and wrongfully
>   accused.
> They said I put false members on my roll.
> I was vilified and slandered, a felon I was branded,
> But I spit on them who poked me in that hole.
>
> I thought the prison lights would blind me, as the
>   door banged shut behind me,
> And they stripped me down and searched me back
>   to front.
> But they couldn't find my make-up, 'cos the
>   bastards weren't awake-up
> To the fact that I'd concealed it in my purse!
>
> They gave me ugly prison issues, and a box of
>   Kleenex tissues
> For to wipe away my tears of bitter grief,
> As I realised all Australia must have seen me as a
>   failure
> And no better than a murderer or thief.

I found the daily grind so hard in the exercising
    yard:
The girls in there were tough as broken glass!
When I tried the snatch and jerk, I couldn't get my
    snatch to work
And I couldn't do a squat to save my arse.

But very soon I would discover that a thief can be
    a mother,
A sister or a daughter or her 'friend',
And a murderer's a victim—just like me, the
    system licked 'em,
When you're close to them they'll touch you in the
    end.

So now I'm proud to call them sisters, even though
    they gave me blisters:
They were much more sympathetic than I thought.
And, unless they were of Asian or Indigenous
    persuasion,
They all came to lean on Pauline for support.

The other material in *Fast and Loose* covered a wide range of small-L liberal issues: corporate excess, the politicisation of the public service, whistleblowers, marginal seat pork-barrelling, the Murdoch empire, the steady demise of the Australian Democrats, the falling water levels in Warragamba Dam and the State Government's feeble response to the crisis. The musical was a *Christmas Carol* version of John Howard's life, from his early days as a trendsetting Young Liberal under the benign influence of Menzies, through the cosy adoration as Bush's 'most obsequious and least effective ally', to his nightmare vision of a future under PM Malcolm Turnbull.

More importantly, it was in *Fast and Loose* that we experimented for the first time with briefly dropping the sugar-coating of laughter. It was Christmas, so, as an encore, we sang in four-part harmony the following simple revision of a well-known carol:

Silent night, violent night.
Baghdad burns, all alight!
Proud we stand at America's side,
Fawning midget along for the ride.
Pride precedeth a fall.
Merry Christmas to all!

Silent night, wary night.
Please repeat, 'She'll be right.'
We hear nothing but slogans and lies.
In this world we do not recognise
Orwell's vision come true.
Merry Christmas to you!

The effect was quite extraordinary. On a high from laughing at the PM in his tartan dressing-gown going down on bended knee before George and Condi, and Malcolm Turnbull pouting in his Ralph Lauren polo knit, the audience was suddenly plunged into a sense of despair beyond anything we had anticipated. A friend remains angry with me to this day for the ease with which we manipulated her emotions. It was a timely reminder of the power of theatre, and of the fact that in the making of effective satire, smiling lips and snarling teeth need not necessarily be incompatible.

2005, April–May:
Concert for Tax Relief

The next *Revue* opened on the sober note struck by our 'Silent Night' finale—or so the opening number asserted:

Welcome, welcome! Welcome one and all!
We're here, you're here, answering the call.
So open up your hearts and let your spirit free,
As we celebrate Australia's new-found generosity.

Welcome, welcome! Glad you've come on board!
Let's choose good news, faith has been restored.
So say goodbye to whingers, show bleeding hearts
  the door.
The *Wharf Revue* is born anew and we will mock
  no more.

'Cos we're satirists for Jesus! And we have seen the
  light,
Not on the hill but in the till, we're moving to the
  right.
And swept up in a tidal wave of love for all
  mankind,
We've turned our backs on smart-arse cracks, left
  ridicule behind.

I once attacked our Government for going to Iraq,
But they've restored democracy, so I'm taking it all
  back.
And I won't call our Prime Minister a brown-nosed
  Yankee puppet,
Who clung so hard to Bush's arse he disappeared
  right up it.

'Cos we're satirists for Jesus! We're swimming with
  the tide,

And when I said Prince Charles gives head, I now
   admit I lied.
The devil made us do it, but we saw through that
   hoax.
It's in the past, we've changed the cast and cut out
   all the jokes.

As 2005 saw the election of the first Iraqi government, it was only natural that we should include a
sketch about the first Iraqi by-election, held minutes
after the winner's declaration from the National
Tally-ban Room. Other segments illustrated how far
we were prepared to go in order to make a political
connection: Margaret and David critiqued the latest
blockbusters out of Canberra, which included Tony
Abbott's star vehicle, *Meet the Focker*, and Kim Jong
Il's North Korean art-house masterpiece, *Crouching
Madman, Hidden Agenda*; art enthusiast Sister
Wendy deconstructed portraits from Old Parliament
House; and nineteenth-century Queensland shearers
discussed enterprise bargaining as a way forward for
the working man.

The musical tackled the emergent Christian 'moral
majority' movement in the Federal Cabinet. Nancy,
now a governess in Dickensian London, is cast out of
her respectable position after falling pregnant to the
master of the house. Unable to keep a job at the local
pub because of her condition, she seeks out Fagin,
who has given up street crime for the more lucrative
profession of backyard abortionist. She is rescued by
the masked guardian of public morality (her former
master, Mr Abbott, although he fails to recognise
her) and delivered to Mr Boswell's Home for Fallen
Women, where she and her unborn child die, despite

the ministrations of an Old Crone. Ever one for the main chance, Mr Abbott recognises an opportunity: give women the vote and the illusion of liberation, and they'll secure him the leadership!

Abortion was never an obvious subject for humour, even of a satirical bent, and the piece met with mixed success. In the light of critical reaction, we modified the ending, but it was a salutary reminder that some issues, despite their manipulation on both sides of the debate for political gain, perhaps still remain outside the purview of revue.

2005–06, November–December, February–March (touring): *Stuff All Happens*

The centrepiece of this, the most recent *Wharf Revue*, was a piece in neo-Elizabethan verse, from the pen of one Julius Marlowe. Entitled *The Damnation of Ruddock*, it represented something of a watershed in our work, certainly a climax in the trend I have been charting, from the light-heartedly comic towards the darkly political and serious. For once, for the first time, we were prepared to go for a good five minutes without a belly laugh!

> *Enter* CHORUS.
>
> CHORUS: Not in the pomp of proud audacious deeds,
> Nor tested on the blood-drenched Fields of Mars,
> He dallied not where hornèd malice feeds
> Ne'er seen as one of Heaven's brightest stars—

Satire—or Sedition?

A moral man who knew his place;
A liberal man, the L of lower case.

A graduate of university,
Conveyancing solicitor for hire.
Pro bono he spoke out for Amnesty,
And thence to politics did he aspire.
His sire in Askin's cabinet did sit,
Till Mr Askin's wife got rid of it.

To Can'b'ra as Berowra's member came
And stood alongside Chaney and McPhee,
Stout Puplick, Baume, their faction wet in
      name—
The human face of liberality.
Now they have gone and he alone here stays,
Collecting stamps to fill his empty days.

> *Exit.*

> RUDDOCK *is revealed at his stamp collection.*

RUDDOCK: Each stamp recalls to me another story
Of battles won and someone else's glory.
My face upon a stamp I'll never see,
While I linger here in anonymity.
And what reward for all my toil and pain?
Defend the poor and poor yourself remain.

No more will I be humble and discreet.
Noble deeds no longer taste so sweet.
Away with human rights and bleeding hearts!
I'll dabble in the necromantic arts.

Come, Lucifer, Old Nick, Beelzebub,
Or some old devil from the Melbourne Club!
Come, sulph'rous imps, your ghoulish forms
      reveal—
Obey my hest, I'm keen to do a deal!

> *A clap of thunder. In a puff of smoke*
> HOWARD *appears.*

45

HOWARD: You summoned me, thou small-L liberal
    wet?
  I'd just prepared the hot tub for Jeanette!
  And eased my Y-fronts down below my knees
  Then oiled the local member for a ...

RUDDOCK: Please!

HOWARD: So, state thy business swift—it best be
    good,
  It's been five years at least since I got wood.

RUDDOCK: This hideous form grim terror will
    inflame.
  I charge thee to return from whence you came!

HOWARD: Oh, what? It took me ages to get into
    this outfit.

RUDDOCK: Begone, foul vision!
  And reappear as young Nick Minchin dressed;
  Such pious shape becomes a devil best.

    Exit HOWARD, *then enter* MICHIN, *talking
    on his mobile phone.*

MINCHIN: Don't worry, mate, we can screw 'im.
  I've got all the dirt to undo 'im.
  Apparently both of them blew 'im.
  Towards me Phil Ruddock is inchin'.
  Better go—see you later. Nick Minchin!

RUDDOCK: Why speakest thou in short, truncated
    verse,
  Each utterance so rude, abrupt and terse?

MINCHIN: I've had a discussion with Peter.
  We're cutting the length of the meter.
  It's quick, cost-efficient and neater.
  And, pending further discussion, we might be
    dropping the rhyming as well.
  John tells me you're wanting promotion.

You know this'll test your devotion.
You wets are a drop in the ocean.
What is the job that you covet?
If it's Finance you want you can shove it.
But Veterans Affairs—you might love it.

RUDDOCK: Too long in junior ministries I've
    wallowed:
    While lesser men have led, I've meekly
    followed.

MINCHIN: Well, assuming an offer comes through,
    Just what do we get out of you?
    I mean, what are you willing to do?

RUDDOCK: My lust for power knows no bounds:
    I'll soon unleash the hellish hounds;
    I'd rip the child from mother's arms;
    And throw them all in prison farms.
    I'd turn back boats on open seas,
    Exclude external territories,
    Drive young men to suicide—
    All pleas for mercy now denied;
    Razor wire, desert's heat,
    Sewn-up lips and shackled feet;
    To decency I'll blind mine eyes,
    And block my ears to children's cries.

MINCHIN: All this you are prepared to be?

RUDDOCK: I'll gladly wear this legacy.
    And I will turn my heart to stone,
    To be the rock on which is grown
    A Liberal victory, owed to me
    And my implacability.

MINCHIN: I reckon you'd be a sensation,
    If you were to run immigration.
    Would that be sufficient temptation?

RUDDOCK: All this I'll surely take on board,
 If I can have as my reward
 Attorney-General—nothing more—
 The lone Protector of the Law.

MINCHIN: So that's your long-term agenda.
 But what do you plan to surrender?

RUDDOCK: I'm putting my soul out to tender.

MINCHIN: Sounds like a bargain to me.
 I expected a much higher fee.
 But if that's what you want it to be …

RUDDOCK: Attorney-General. Nothing higher,
 There's nothing more that I desire.

MINCHIN: Best if that's just left unspoken—
 Promises are easily broken.
 Your fly's undone! Only jokin'!

  Exit.

  Enter CHORUS.

CHORUS: So wily Ruddock to his word was true
 And stood with Reith as truth went overboard;
 In *Tampa*'s wake he steered his party through,
 His place beside his master now assured.

The borders shut, as iron walls descended
Against poor souls left stateless and adrift.
Unburdened by his soul, he now ascended,
Unshaken by a public family rift.

And eyes that once on tenderness reflected,
Now blankly, lizard-like, unblinking stared.
Incompetence, concealed, went undetected,
While lawyer's tongue lashed anyone who cared.

The nation's heart he poisoned and besmirched.
Our reputation lowered by the year,
As further down the slippery slope we lurched,
All decency now silenced by our fear.

As he stepped across the carcass of Australia
To the office he had long and keenly sought,
His victory, this country's moral failure.
But was that victory far too dearly bought?

RUDDOCK: Oh, the days are long, the nights are
        cold ...
But what is this that doth my conscience prick?
From Amnesty, the pin I wore of old.
And yet no blood flows—what is this trick?

A heartless Nosferatu am I now,
Doomed to sit in office for all time?
But, pah! That's all I wanted anyhow.
I take the view that it's been worth the climb.

        Re-enter MINCHIN.

MINCHIN: I've come to collect on the bargain,
So none of your legalese jargon!
I realise you're now on a roll,
But it's time to surrender your soul.

RUDDOCK: With all respect, it's my view that, after
a detailed and comprehensive analysis of the
documentation forwarded by your department,
it would be deemed prudent to conclude
that the contractual obligations are open to
interpretation.

My soul I leased—sole ownership remains
My property and safe from Hell's domains.

        Another clap of thunder.

MINCHIN: The devil you've done like a dinner.
We thought we were on to a winner—
You were our number-one sinner.

You think you're so fuckin' clever!
This lease with the devil's forever:
It's a contract that no one can sever!

RUDDOCK: To Hell with you and your infernal sport!

MINCHIN: I'll see you yet in Hell!

RUDDOCK: No. I'll see you in court!

    Another clap of thunder.

ALL: [*singing*] Truth perverted;
    Faust inverted;
    Satan routed by the law.

RUDDOCK: The table's turned,
    The devil spurned
    And he may not collect me.

    I stay intact;
    I changed the Act
    To let the law protect me.

ALL: The law's intent
    Can soon be bent—
    And thus did I/he construe it.

    I/he tempted fate;
    It took the bait;
    The devil made me/him do it.

    But nothing's free—
    This victory
    Has left him gaunt and pallid.

    The living dead
    All feeling fled
    To keep this contract valid.

    He may not dwell
    In fiery Hell,
    But Hell now burns within him.

    Yet who's to blame?
    We share the shame,
    Because we let him do his damn'dest in our
        name.

The rest of the show was a grab-bag of Amanda Vanstone; *The Latham Diaries*, adapted into a contemporary song-cycle by Dorothy Porter and young composer Helena Yatschernin Cockington-twats; Alexander Downer, doing a variety turn at the end of the APEC Conference; our two ardent Australian Democrat supporters, contemplating the direct action of street protest; and, for the musical finale, a tribute to 'affluenza', our society's rampant consumerism.

For the first time the show toured outside the metropolitan area into regional NSW, to Victoria, to Hobart and, for one big night, to Bunbury, WA. We were delighted, though hardly surprised, to discover that the audience's appetite for political material was just as enthusiastic elsewhere as in Sydney: even in conservative electorates there was a willingness to shake a rusty lance at the creaking windmill our parlous democracy had become. Like the converse image in the mirror held up to nature, it seemed that the more mean-spirited the times became, the more desperate became the need to laugh about them.

Seditious Intent?

*S*tuff *All Happens* opened in a torrid political climate, created by John Howard's announcement on 27 September 2005 that he was proposing changes to the existing statutes on sedition and seditious intent, changes which were designed as part of the Federal Government's new Anti-terrorism Bill. Within days of the Bill's introduction, a broad coalition of artists, performers, journalists, publishers and civil libertarians condemned the proposed laws as a threat to free speech. Why, they asked, were the existing sedition laws, last used in this country in the early 1960s and effectively defunct ever since, being revitalised at a time when practically every other Western democracy had removed the crime of sedition from their statutes?

A majority Senate committee report into the Anti-terrorism Bill recommended—one of 52 proposed changes—that the sedition provisions be removed until after a review, believing that they were poorly drafted, undermined free speech and that the existing law negated any urgency for their introduction. The Federal Attorney-General, Philip Ruddock, dismissed the recommendations, but promised that the laws would be reviewed after they were introduced.

His assurances did little to dampen opposition. What most worried those artists concerned with freedom of expression was Schedule 7, particularly Section 30A, which defined 'seditious intention' as:

an intention to effect any of the following
purposes:

> (a) to bring the Sovereign into hatred or
>   contempt;
> (b) to urge disaffection against the following:
>> (i) the Constitution;
>> (ii) the Government of the
>>   Commonwealth;
>> (iii) either House of the Parliament;
> (c) to urge another person to attempt,
>   otherwise than by lawful means, to procure
>   a change to any matter established by law in
>   the Commonwealth;
> (d) to promote feelings of ill-will or hostility
>   between different groups so as to threaten
>   the peace, order and good government of
>   the Commonwealth.

Obviously, clauses (a) and (b) could have an enormous
impact on anyone performing satire. The *Wharf Revue*
had done little else but 'urge disaffection against [...]
the Government' for the last six years! More importantly, in the words of Spencer Zifcak, an associate
professor of law at La Trobe University, the proposed
sedition laws represented the 'outlawing of words
[and] the criminalisation of speech'.[6]

In early November 2005, comedian and broadcaster
Wendy Harmer joined forces with José Borghino,
editor of the *New Matilda* webmagazine, to stage an
anti-sedition concert at the Sydney Theatre in Walsh
Bay. The STC donated the venue and the *Wharf Revue*
was invited to participate, along with performers like
Eddy Perfect, Max Gillies, Gerry Connolly, *The Chaser*
team, Wil Anderson, Andrew Denton and various

more formal speakers. Within seven days of going on sale, tickets were completely sold out. And, despite being nearly four hours long, the concert, which was held on 13 November, was hugely successful.[7] It formed a small part of a wider campaign fought by organisations such as MEAA, the Australian Writers Guild, the National Association for the Visual Arts, Australian Lawyers for Human Rights and major media companies including News Limited and Fairfax, to name but a few.

The campaign had some success. Bowing to the pressure, the Government inserted five vital words into Section 30A. It was revised to read:

> Seditious intention means an intention *to use force or violence* to effect any of the following purposes ...

It was now safe for Gerry Connolly to continue impersonating the Queen without the threat of arrest putting him off a refreshing beverage after the show; it was alright for the *Wharf Revue* to continue urging disaffection against the Government—just as long as we stopped short of planning its violent overthrow. Or was it?

Section 80.2 of the Schedule deals with sedition itself and reads as follows:

> (1) A person commits an offence if the person urges another person to overthrow by force or violence:
>> (a) the Constitution; or
>> (b) the Government of the Commonwealth, a State or a Territory; or
>> (c) the lawful authority of the Government of the Commonwealth.
>
> Penalty: Imprisonment for 7 years.

(2) Recklessness applies to paragraphs 1(a), (b)
   and (c).

The law as currently drafted does not require proof of
a real probability of violence flowing from the words
as a necessary element of the offence. It's possible
that someone may interpret your words or actions in
a way that you never for a moment intended. Peter
Gray SC, in legal advice given to the Opposition Arts
spokesman Peter Garrett MP, wrote:

> Such 'urging' is not defined in the Bill or the
> Criminal Code [... T]he term need not by any
> means be restricted to positive or express recom-
> mendation or persuasion, but could for example
> extend to cover indirect 'urging' by way of analogy,
> or dramatisation, or imagery, or metaphor, or al-
> legory, or allusion or any of the myriad devices and
> techniques available to a creative artist.[8]

Simeon Beckett, President of Australian Lawyers for
Human Rights, points out that 'artists and galleries
which show their work are vulnerable to being
prosecuted for influencing others, whether this was
intended or not'.[9] The same may be said for satirists,
particularly in the theatre, where dramatic irony, a
notoriously tricky device for some audience members
to read, is heavily employed.

The concept of recklessness is another grey area.
Under the usually accepted legal definition, 'recklessness' implies a decision to proceed despite a reasonable
knowledge of the risk involved. This is a much lower
threshold than intention to commit an offence.

Again, it's tricky for a theatre practitioner. How can
you possibly know who all your audience members are

going to be? How can you second-guess the cultural or psychological profiles of your audience and tailor your material to avoid the risk of being misinterpreted?

Writing for the Arts Law Centre of Australia Online, Deborah Doctor concluded that

> the potential for the new provisions to be used to stifle free speech is evident with respect to creative works, including artistic works, films and literary works that are satirical or metaphoric. Often an artist is providing some social commentary or criticism in their work and their work may be open to multiple subjective responses. For example, [...] an artist might be accused of being responsible for urging another person to commit offences, as a result of a person interpreting their artwork in a particular way, even if this interpretation was unintended.[10]

Furthermore, paragraph (7) in part reads:

> A person commits an offence if:
>
>   (a) the person urges another person to engage in conduct; and
>
>   (b) the first-mentioned person intends the conduct to assist, by any means whatever, an organisation or country; and
>
>   (c) the organisation or country is:
>
>   (i) at war with the Commonwealth, whether or not the existence of a state of war has been declared

The Attorney-General agreed to drop the phrase 'by any means whatever', but it still leaves the definition of 'intention' vague. Under this drafting of the law, simple opposition to an act of war—even as yet undeclared—could be interpreted as assisting the organisation or country that is the target of the act of war. Performing a sketch that sympathetically portrayed the struggle of the Iraqi resistance movement or brought the occupying forces into disrepute could also be so construed.

The defences provided by the Act against these charges are as narrow as the definitions of the offences are broad. Humanitarian aid is exempt, but the defendant bears the evidential burden: s/he has to prove her/his innocence. Other offences within Section 80.2 carry a defence of 'good faith' and anyone pointing out errors or defects in the government, sovereign or parliaments of the Commonwealth in good faith is asked once more to bear the evidential burden.

But what exactly is 'good faith'? Can it be an act of naivety, or does the term imply some measure of consideration and clarity of purpose? In considering such a defence, the court may have regard to any relevant matter, including whether the acts were done 'for a purpose intended to be prejudicial to the safety or defence of the Commonwealth'. One person's good faith may easily be another's purpose intended to be prejudicial to the good order of the nation.

So, why has the Government gone down this path? The obvious targets of sedition laws are the religious extremists who preach a path of violence from whatever pulpit they occupy, although—let's be honest—at this moment in time, the laws are aimed squarely at the extremist imams advocating jihad against the West, and Australia in particular. Many would argue that the current climate of fear and paranoia has presented a golden opportunity for governments to clamp down on any form of dissent or questioning. But, even leaving such theories aside, it's plain that the haste with which the laws were introduced has made the sedition provisions a very wide catch-all driftnet indeed.

The changes already made to Schedule 7 suggest that the Government has conceded this point, but their reluctance to alter the next schedule and the introduction into the sedition laws of the concepts of 'urging' and 'recklessness' indicate that the alarm bells being rung by civil libertarians are anything but false.

So, what does the potential prosecution of the sedition laws mean to the likes of the *Wharf Revue* and the freedom of theatre-makers generally? In the balance of probability, not a great deal. The new laws pose a far greater threat to journalists and publishers, who are understandably concerned about the threat to free speech and other provisions buried within the Anti-terrorism Bill. The most serious threat to performing artists lay in Schedule 7, but the insertion of the phrase 'to use force or violence' has largely blunted it. And, although Schedule 8 could be brought to bear against our particular brand of satire, it's doubtful that our attacks on the Government could be reasonably construed as urging others to act against the Constitution or the national interest.

That said, if you are, say, an Islamic comedian in this country, you have every right to be worried. The *Wharf Revue* has always operated within the mainstream, while historically sedition has been used on ideological grounds as an instrument of social control against those outside it. For example, we operate within socially acceptable parameters, such as recognising the legal supremacy of secular authority. A satirist arguing for a different set of beliefs could face prosecution. Like all humour, satire is subjective and the laws' nebulous definitions, exacerbated by the fact that there need be no proof of a causal link between the deemed 'urging' and the 'urged', give the authorities an unnecessarily strong hand.

Which brings me to the Australian Law Reform Commission (ALRC) review of the laws, requested by the Attorney-General and, at the time of writing (June 2006), released as a discussion paper prior to finalisation and submission to the Government. Professor David Weisbrot, President of the ALRC, said:

> Australians place a very high value on free speech and robust political debate. There is no reason why these offences, which properly target the urging of force or violence, cannot be framed in such a way to avoid capturing dissenting views and opinions or stifling the work of journalists, cartoonists, artists and film-makers either directly or through the 'chilling effect' of self-censorship.[11]

Indeed, I believe the greatest and most immediate threat in the existing laws lies in that 'chilling' self-censorship, and agree with Edward Albee, one of the theatre's staunchest supporters of the artist's right to freedom of speech. 'The censorship we impose on ourselves,' he said, 'is more insidious [than any government censorship]. You should be holding a mirror up to people and saying, "This is the way you behave and, if you don't like it, you should change."'[12] Furthermore, organisations that rely on government subsidy—and there are few professional arts bodies in this country that do not to some extent rely on it—may be wary of programming or commissioning works that could be construed as seditious and therefore liable to put their funding in jeopardy. Also of concern would be the potentially prohibitive expense of defending such allegations.

The *Wharf Revue*, although part of the STC, is independently viable and not subsidised out of general revenue. General Manager Rob Brookman points out that there has been no issue with political content from any of the funding bodies and that the company's 'stand against sedition was more [a matter of] principle than [provoked by] any perceived implication for operations'. Hannie Rayson's play, *Two Brothers*, which deals with a fictional pair of siblings bearing an uncanny resemblance to Federal Treasurer Peter Costello and his brother Tim, had a much higher political profile and caused its producers, the Melbourne and Sydney Theatre Companies, considerably greater problems than anything in six years of *Wharf Revues*. Government disapproval was articulated to the point where the Chair of the Melbourne Theatre Company, Ian Rennard, was contacted by the Federal Minister for the Arts and asked, 'Why do you bite the hand that feeds you?'

But bear in mind that that particular incident of political interference occurred in early 2005, before the drafting of the sedition laws. How much more likely that in a heightened atmosphere of suspicion such calls could become more commonplace? And, if vigorous prosecution under the present democratic tolerance enjoyed by this country seems unlikely, future governments may be even less benign than the current one. Traditionally, all wedges have at least one thin edge.

So how does the ALRC propose to counter this problem? First, by removing the notion of 'sedition' from the statutes. Professor Weisbrot again:

> Given its history, the term 'sedition' is much too closely associated in the public mind with punishment of those who criticise the established order. [...] The new offences in s80.2 of the *Criminal Code* [... are] really just another form of the longstanding offence of incitement to violence. Continued use of the term 'sedition' only confuses the issues.[13]

Semantic nicety? The essence of the criminal offence remains largely the same. However, if the further 25 proposals for reform mooted by the ALRC are pursued, artists and performers will be afforded some safeguards. Most importantly, the Commission goes on to suggest that

> [t]he provisions need amendment to make clear that the Crown must prove beyond reasonable doubt that the person *intentionally* urged others to use force or violence, and intended that this force or violence would occur. We also propose that in applying the law to a particular case, the jury must take into account the context in which the conduct occurred, such as whether it was part of an artistic performance or exhibition, or a genuine academic, artistic or scientific discussion, or an industrial dispute, or in a news report or commentary about a matter of public interest.[14]

However, this approach has some problems. The defence of artistic licence has been challenged many times in this country. The very interpretation of what constitutes 'art' has long been contentious. For example, the recent case brought against 2004 Archibald Prize-winner Craig Ruddy hinged on whether or not his entry constituted a 'painting' or a 'drawing'. The presiding NSW Supreme Court Judge, Justice John Hamilton, commented, 'There is a certain appearance of strangeness in courts making determinations concerning the qualities of works of art. The matter is better left to those in the art world.'[15]

How then can we confidently expect a court to define terms such as 'artistic performance or exhibition' or 'genuine artistic discussion'. Or, indeed, 'commentary about a matter of public interest'? Might not one man's commentary very easily be another's polemic? And, of course, the ALRC's reforms are only suggestions. The Government could easily ignore them, and any law that remains on the statutes may be 'reviewed' at any convenient time.

Legal definitions aside, Stephen Armstrong thinks there might be a problem, if an audience were to regard material put before it as seditious. In an atmosphere charged with threat and suspicion, audiences are hardly likely to wish to be thought unpatriotic. A long bow, perhaps, but for more mainstream companies it could be a consideration that affects their programming decisions. The effect has certainly been felt in America. After his Nobel lecture last year, in which he railed against US foreign policy and branded the invasion of Iraq 'a bandit act, an act of blatant state terrorism', Harold Pinter quickly found that his plays had become an endangered species in US theatres.[16] Revue, however, enjoys the advantage of not being ideologically driven. The general perception is that everyone is a target for its barbs.

A further implication of self-censorship in the modern age of terrorism is the reluctance on the part of both artists and managements to present material that may provoke a response from those extremist elements that the sedition laws are supposedly intended to suppress. Threats against personal safety can have a dampening effect on one's enthusiasm to turn a spotlight onto radical Islam, for example. Stage productions have already been cancelled in Britain because of death threats against the box-office staff. Call me cowardly, if you will, but, having once been involved twenty years ago in a satirical programme that incurred the anger of a hardline Middle-Eastern state, I shall not be pushing to the front of the line to repeat the experiment!

Yet, for all the talk of sedition, the most pressing obstacle to freedom of satirical expression comes from defamation laws. At the beginning of 2006 the differing state laws were unified on a national basis—except in the case of Tasmania, where it is still possible to defame the dead—and altered slightly in favour of publishers and producers: whereas previously truth as a defence had to be proven in the public interest, now truth is in itself a defence. A limit has been set on damages and the action must now be brought within a year of publication or production. Even so, the per-capita incidence of defamation is higher in Sydney than in London or New York. The mere receipt of a solicitor's letter threatening a defamation suit is usually sufficient to have the material in question censored, because the cost of continuing the correspondence, let alone defending the action, is simply prohibitive.

Over the course of a long career Max Gillies has been the target of several defamation suits, notably from the late Kerry Packer, who objected to a sketch on *The Gillies Report* that linked him to allegations made in a Federal inquiry. That case was prosecuted in the ACT, the Territory's defamation laws at the time being seen as potentially the most lucrative for the complainant. Gillies regards defamation as a problem because it is in the nature of the satirist's job to be derogatory about public figures; comic effect demands distortion, and characterisation is often driven by inference or implication that is, shall we say, unflattering. But the more sensitive amongst us will only grant the Fool a certain licence, and there are some high-profile media identities who keep their reputations intact through the aggressive threat of defamation action. Ironically, they are often the most successfully and frequently sued defendants of defamation themselves—happy to dish it out, but none too thrilled to take it!

Closing Number

In conclusion, I should like to reflect on the relatively healthy state of satire on the contemporary Australian stage. While its profile may be modest, the revue form works and can attract an audience. While the relevance of theatre is frequently questioned, the growing demand for the *Wharf Revue* and others like it demonstrates that the theatre is still capable of responding with immediacy and effectiveness to contemporary events and issues. Ducking artfully behind the ambiguous screen of 'It's just a joke, mate', revue can deliver sharper blows than more serious forms of art or media, and so contribute to a broader social awareness that might ultimately work to bring about political change. Although the charge of being too 'mainstream' or 'bourgeois' has been levelled at the *Wharf Revue*, the irony is that our work would seem to appeal to the demographic most fit and best placed to effect political change.

The *Revue* offers an oppositional point of view to a political process that is increasingly removed from its constituents. The devaluation of parliament and our democratic institutions that has continued apace in the last decade has left the electorate largely cynical and uninterested. Good satire can reawaken a desire for change, because in the hearts of all satirists is a belief in the worth of the institutions and customs they regard as being mismanaged, or, even worse, degraded or corrupt.

The revision of the sedition clauses of the Anti-terrorism Bill has undoubtedly compromised freedom of speech in this country. However, the amended legislation poses little direct threat to the ability of satirists to speak their minds. If the reforms proposed by the ALRC are adopted, that threat is further diminished. In all likelihood, such freedom as we enjoy derives more from the fact that comedians are never as greatly feared as journalists and writers. Humour, after all, is the refuge of the vanquished, rarely the conqueror. A far greater restraint on our freedom of speech is the censorship that arts organisations or corporations will impose upon themselves, in order to avoid falling foul of the new legislation and the threat of defamation that already exists.

Not that we harbour any illusions about our capacity to change the world. Back in 1998, the satirist John Clarke said on ABC radio:

> There is, I suppose, a fear with satire that all it does is keep people amused, while the system gets worse and worse and worse. [...] I mean, satirists are really just doing certain things, but they're not on the bridge, they're not steering the ship, and I don't know that they can. And they are in great danger of becoming the band who plays 'Abide with Me' while the thing sinks. Theoretically, I think.[17]

Personally, I would be disguising myself as a woman and clamouring for the lifeboats, but I do take his point. And I've always borne in mind the words of Peter Cook, who described his political revue club, The Establishment, in London as 'a satirical venue [after the fashion of] those wonderful Berlin cabarets that did so much to stop the rise of Hitler and prevent the outbreak of the Second World War'.[18]

But then again, even the converted need to be occasionally preached to and reminded of why they converted in the first place.

Appendix

List of Writers and Performers of the *Wharf Revue*, 2000–2006

2000, February–March
The End of the Wharf as We Know It
> Cast: Jonathan Biggins, Drew Forsythe, Linda Nagle & Phil Scott
> Writers: The cast

2000, August–September
The Unofficial Visitors' Guide to Australia
> Cast: Jonathan Biggins, Drew Forsythe, Andrew Ross & Jacki Weaver
> Writers: Jonathan Biggins, Carl Caulfield, Patrick Cook, Drew Forsythe, Linda Nagle, Andrew Ross, Phil Scott, Stephen Sewell & David Williamson

2000, November–December
Beyond Our Control
> Cast: Robyn Moase, Andrew Ross, Tony Sheldon & Tony Taylor
> Writers: The cast

2001, March–April
Free Petrol
Cast: Valerie Bader, Jonathan Biggins, Drew
 Forsythe & Phil Scott
Writers: Jonathan Biggins, Drew Forsythe, Phil
 Scott, Angus FitzSimons & Rachael Spratt

2001, August–September
Free Petrol, Too!
Cast: Valerie Bader, Jonathan Biggins, Drew
 Forsythe & Phil Scott
Writers: Jonathan Biggins, Drew Forsythe & Phil
 Scott

2002, March–April
The Year of Living Comfortably
Cast: Valerie Bader, Drew Forsythe, Phil Scott &
 Tony Sheldon
Writers: Jonathan Biggins, Drew Forsythe, Phil
 Scott, Tony Sheldon, Linda Nagle & Patrick
 Cook

2002, November–December
Much Revue About Nothing
Cast: Jonathan Biggins, Drew Forsythe, Linda
 Nagle & Phil Scott
Writers: The cast

2003, June–August
Sunday in Iraq with George
Cast: Valerie Bader, Jonathan Biggins, Phil Scott &
 Tony Sheldon
Writers: Jonathan Biggins, Phil Scott, Tony
 Sheldon, Linda Nagle & Drew Forsythe

2004, November–December
Fast and Loose
> Cast: Jonathan Biggins, Drew Forsythe, Genevieve
> Lemon & Phil Scott.
> Writers: Jonathan Biggins, Drew Forsythe & Phil
> Scott

2005, April–May
Concert for Tax Relief
> Cast: Jonathan Biggins, Michelle Doake, Garry
> Scale & Phil Scott
> Writers: Jonathan Biggins, Phil Scott & Drew
> Forsythe

2005–06, November–December, February–March (touring)
Stuff All Happens
> Cast: Jonathan Biggins, Drew Forsythe, Genevieve
> Lemon & Phil Scott
> Writers: Jonathan Biggins, Drew Forsythe & Phil
> Scott

Endnotes

1   *Beyond the Fringe*, which in 1963 included Peter Cook's celebrated impersonation of serving British Prime Minister Harold Macmillan, was said to have been the first show in living memory to publicly mock politicians, churchmen and the armed forces.

2   Philippa Wherrett, 'Political bunfight', at http://www.theblurb.com.au/Issue60/StuffAllHappens.htm (accessed 28 June 2006).

3   For cast lists and writing credits, see the Appendix, p. 67.

4   'Beyond a Joke', *Background Briefing*, ABC Radio National, 15 February 1998, transcript, at http://abc.net.au/rn/backgroundbriefing/stories/1998/10504.htm (accessed 28 June 2006).

5   'Beyond a Joke', transcript.

6   Quoted in 'Sedition! The Anti-Terrorism Laws and the threat to free expression', *Lingua Franca*, ABC Radio National, 4 March 2006, transcript, at www.abc.net.au/rn/linguafranca/stories/2006/1582440.htm (accessed 28 June 2006).

7   A repeat performance was given in Melbourne the following month, but with a modified line-up of participants.

8   'Advice [...], 28 October 2005', at www.vicpeace.org/sedition/info/0002.html (accessed 28 June 2006).

9   Quoted in 'New sedition law to stifle artists', 3

November 2005, at www.craftaustralia.com.au/articles/20051103.php (accessed 28 June 2006).

10 Quoted in 'Sedition and the Arts', at www.artslaw.com.au/ArtLaw/Current/06SeditionAndTheArts.asp (accessed 28 June 2006).

11 Quoted in a media release entitled '"Sedition"should go, focus on urging violence', 29 May 2006, at www.alrc.gov.au/media/2006/mr2905.htm (accessed 28 June 2006).

12 Quoted by Chris Evans, 'Edward Albee—always uncensored' (21 May 2001), at http://www.freedomforum.org/templates/document.asp?documentID=13973 (accessed 28 June 2006).

13 ALRC media release, '"Sedition" should go'

14 Quoted in *Review of Sedition Laws: Discussion Paper 71* (May 2006), at www.austlii.edu.au/au/other/alrc/publications/dp/71/ (accessed 28 June 2006).

15 Quoted by Natasha Wallace, 'Hung, drawn and slaughtered: art dispute gets brush off', *Sydney Morning Herald*, 15 June 2006.

16 'Art, truth and politics', transcript, at http:/nobel prize.org/nobel_prizes/literature/laureates/2005/   pinter-lecture-e.html (accessed 29 June 2006).

17 'Beyond a Joke', transcript.

18 Quoted in an obituary entitled 'The man who invented British satire', at http://www.petercook.net/articles/telegraph-1.htm (accessed 29 June 2006).

Readers' Forum

Response to Amanda Card's Platform Papers No. 8, *Body for Hire?: The State of Dance in Australia*

Erin Brannigan works in the fields of dance and film as an academic, curator and journalist.

Albeit belated, this response to Amanda Card's essay is opportune. As I write, Graeme Murphy and Janet Vernon have just announced their intention to resign after thirty years in their positions as artistic directors of Sydney Dance Company (SDCo), Australia's flagship contemporary dance company. They will leave on 1 April 2007. Card's comprehensive and incisive survey of the state of dance in Australia will soon, with some good luck and savvy decision-making, be superseded, as the field undergoes a seismic shift from the top down over the next two years. Choreographer-led flagship companies will be revealed as unsustainable in this cultural and political climate, a fact which has clearly made a pre-emptive strike at Murphy and Vernon. Resources have to be shared, a belief that discreetly underpins Card's arguments. It is to be hoped that SDCo will make the smart move and change to a more open, widely supportive company with a flexible stable of dancers working with Australian and international choreographers and overseen by a creative director. Moreover, this improved structure would revitalise the company's image and provide infrastructure for more artists.

72

It would also be a more equitable structure. In New South Wales, SDCo has kept its funds, and more importantly, its audiences to itself. Under Graeme Murphy, SDCo has cut itself off from the local dance community and lost relevance within the broader cultural landscape. This has not been the case with other flagship companies such as Australian Dance Theatre, Bangarra Dance Theatre, or Chunky Move, who all, in a variety of ways, support local choreographers, whether emergent or established. Like Murphy—for whom all of them have worked—Stephen Page, Garry Stewart and Gideon Obarzanek landed their current positions when they only had a few full-length works under their dance belts. They have built up local support as they have developed as choreographers, creating an artistic and public profile and gaining all the attendant benefits and responsibilities. But they have been careful to share their resources. They have adapted just enough to guarantee their survival. The same cannot be said of SDCo.

For Card, the current problems with the dance scene have everything to do with the structure of the flagship contemporary companies. (She replaces Bangarra and Chunky Move with Expressions, Danceworks, Tasdance and Buzz Dance Theatre to create a state-by-state list.) Card believes the main problem with choreographer-led companies is that they place an unnecessarily heavy emphasis on the 'auteur' and give insufficient credit to the dancers as collaborators. She is spot-on, but only for very limited cases. Perhaps it's stating the obvious, but only in theory can a 'dictatorial' and a 'democratic' approach to ensemble choreography be seen as mutually exclusive alternatives. In the reality of the dance studio the creative process is as complex and varied as the artists themselves.

Card's alternative model of state companies made up of 'bodies for hire' is a radical provocation, reducing the role of the choreographer at the expense of giving the dancer job security. Handing the company structures over to the dancers and rotating the choreographers is not a viable option. Of the choreographers associated with Card's Super Group of dancers (which, by its very nature, is an unfairly exclusive list), there is not one who would, or could, relinquish their right to choose their own mix of performers in order to realise a personal artistic vision. It is the choreographer's artistic vision that is ultimately devalued in this model: Card's claim of a current 'homogenisation' of choreographic invention across the companies working with the Super Group of dancers, due to the dancers' overwhelming input into movement development, is her most damning and controversial criticism (p. 32). And what about the dancer's right to choose creative directors?

Which brings us back to the problem that SDCo must soon face: who will take up the company of dancers as they now stand, hand-picked by Murphy and Vernon? Garry Stewart? Gideon Obarzanek? Or, perhaps, Kate Champion? Or Meryl Tankard? The SDCo dancers are perfectly suited to Murphy's aesthetics, but would not be right for these other choreographers. Whatever the change, it will be radical—and welcome. Create better equity and security with the limited resources available and let the artists—choreographers, dancers and other collaborators—find each other. And on this note, Amanda Card was right about an essential point in her argument on behalf of the dancer: more open auditions by dance companies would also be a welcome change.

Responses to Stuart Cunningham's Platform Papers No. 9, *What Price a Creative Economy?*

Martin Hirst teaches in the School of Communications and Contemporary Arts at Edith Cowan University. With John Harrison, he is the author of *Communication and New Media: Broadcast to Narrowcast* (OUP, forthcoming).

Critical analysis is in short supply in Stuart Cunningham's essay. There is little mention of the culturally negative effects of the further commodification of leisure, pleasure and popular culture when capitalism pushes its mantra of accumulation into the 'arts'.

The working definition of 'creative industries' is broad and loose. For example, does the category of 'designer fashion' include heavily branded clothing, footwear and accessories produced under industrial sweatshop conditions in Southeast Asia, Mexico and China?

Raymond Williams pioneered the critical investigation of popular culture and 'creative' industries in his studies of television, theatre, literature and other cultural forms almost 40 years ago. His work, grounded in political economy and materialism, is still relevant. But Williams is ignored here in favour of Richard Florida's 'creative class' thesis and the apologetic theorists of neo-classical economics who have been unable to properly explain the real world since they abandoned Keynes for Freidman.

However, there are some important clues in Cunningham's argument. He is right to point to the need of capital in Australia (and indeed globally) to harness cultural production to an 'industry policy framework' (p. 11). The question to be asked is 'why?'

The answers only make sense if they are related to the political economy of creative industries, rather than an econometric accounting. A critical approach will make use of Manuel Castells's 'mode of development' thesis in his *Rise of the Network Society* (1996). The 'mode of development' is the historically specific ensemble of methods that capitalism adopts in relation to particular technologies and areas of value to organise its ongoing renewal of profitability. It is this dialectic of combined and uneven development that gives capitalism its resilience.

The first example is the British government's definition of 'creative industries': 'the potential for wealth and job creation through the generation and exploitation of intellectual property' (cited on p. 5). Why is this necessary in the first decade of the twenty-first century? If one looks at the work of Castells and other political economists of communication the answer is fairly obvious.

Capitalism needs to continuously regenerate its sources of surplus value, accumulation and profit. The declining global rate of profit (the tendency towards periodic crises in accumulation) is exacerbated by the rising organic composition of capital—that is, 'dead labour' replaces 'living labour' as machines replace human beings in the production process—causing a further decline in productivity (as measured by the extraction of surplus value). Faced with these periodic crises, the capitalist economy seeks new areas to colonise and, as Williams pointed out in *Problems in Materialism and Culture* (1980), for the past 50 years popular culture has been a site of increasing commodification and surplus value. The 'creative economy' is a descriptor for the ways in which capitalism is seeking to renew its profitability by commodifying many aspects of the digital production of culture.

The use of the Chinese example of creative 'renewal' (pp. 8–9) is also instructive. If one assumes that China is somehow a post-capitalist society it doesn't make sense, but if we assume it is a capitalist economy (state-capitalism with a growing class of private capitalists) then its efforts to harness creativity to profitability are merely symptomatic of China's attempts to integrate itself with global capitalism. China has learned from Japan, Taiwan and Korea who have already adopted the networked society mode of development (see Castells).

My final example is the 'techno-legal time gap' that develops between application and regulation as global capitalism attempts to realign intellectual property regimes to 'keep pace with technological and social change' (p. 13). It is necessary to realign bourgeois property and production relations in favour of capital to ensure the continuing accumulation of surplus value.

It is unfortunate that Cunningham makes no attempt to engage with the critical dimensions of this debate. It is less a personal failing than a symptom of the failure of Australia's critical intellectuals to engage with a political economy analysis. Instead, some scholars are content to describe ideological constructs such as 'creative industries' and the 'knowledge economy', ignoring the tough questions.

What price a creative economy? The continuation of global capitalism, the further marginalisation of dissent as popular culture becomes more homogenous and commoditised and the continued exploitation of 'creatives' as they are chewed up and spat out of the great maw of 'industry'.

Benjamin Marks is co-author, together with Rodney Marks and Robert Spillane, of *The Management Contradictionary* (South Yarra: Michelle Anderson Publishing, 2006).

I fully agree with the general thrust of Stuart Cunningham's essay: 'The "price" to be paid [for a creative economy] is that the special status attributed to the arts and culture is folded into the need for creativity across the economy and society. To reach our destination, we must take the long way round' (p. 44). But this is the only point on which we agree. We both want a creative economy, but Cunningham's 'long way round' to get it is too narrow for my liking.

Instead of analysing government involvement in the arts, he acknowledges that old arguments do not work, that new ones are needed and that, compared to some other industries, the arts do not receive anywhere near as much funding or immunity from criticism. So what!?

Cunningham agrees with John Holden, author of *Capturing Cultural Value: How Culture has become a Tool of Government Policy* (2004), when he says that 'no one speaks of the "subsidised" defence industry, the "mendicant" education sector or a health system "propped up" by government funding. Yet all these sectors are funded substantially or wholly by our tax dollars and are subject to the same supposed regime of market failure as the arts and culture' (p. 3). This hardly addresses the question of whether government funding of the arts (including indirect funding) is justified. It is an argument based on popularity rather than logic. It is understandable that one might draw a comparison between government funding of defence, education and health, which is widely accepted, and the arts, which is more controversial. But, what if someone—such as myself, for example—were to come along who doubted that government should subsidise defence, education and health services? I contend that government intervention must prevent competition, which is, after all, what it is designed to do. This tends to result in the end product being of inferior quality and higher cost than if government did not intervene. This is basic economics. Either economics is a science and the law of supply and demand always true, or it is not. Cunningham does not believe that economics is a science.

He makes no attempt to defend his claim that because 'the electromagnetic spectrum [is] a scarce public resource' (p. 25), government involvement is necessary. All economic goods are by definition scarce, and what exactly does he mean here by 'public'? Surely, economic goods can only be private; the real question is whether or not owning them is criminal. Whether they are distributed effectively is not a scientific question, because the judge of efficiency is utility, which is not inter-subjectively comparable. What is the unit of measurement for 'utility'?

Interestingly, Cunningham doesn't invariably choose to enclose the word 'price' in inverted commas. This is because a price is something that is voluntarily agreed upon, whereas a cost is something foregone. Cost does not determine price. Suppose someone lives in seclusion, spends their lifetime reinventing the wheel and then looks to be reimbursed for the time and effort that this has cost them. Who would they sue if they weren't? Disambiguation of cost and price is central to any economic analysis. Where government is involved, either there are no prices, or else prices are grossly distorted. Government by definition uses force to extract its income, and therefore there are no prices (which by definition must be voluntarily agreed upon) attached to government interference, only costs. The difference in connotation is clear.

Cunningham admits that the traditional—albeit fallacious—argument from market failure to justification of government fails. However, instead of advocating the cessation of government involvement, he wishes to be 'pragmatic' and 'keep moving forward on several fronts, lest [he] be outflanked or forced into retreat' (p. 44), i.e. challenged or refuted. He suggests that '[s]everal bodies of economic thought need to be tapped to engage this challenge, among them transaction-cost economics, growth theory, and evolutionary and information economics. This process has only begun' (p. 33). Back in 1967, in their *Social Construction of Reality*, p. 128, Peter Berger and Thomas Luckmann wrote the following prescient words: 'It is correct to say that theories are concocted in order to legitimate already existing social institutions.' It is peculiar that Cunningham himself lacks the ingenuity and faith in the arts that he is anxious to foster in others.